Colors

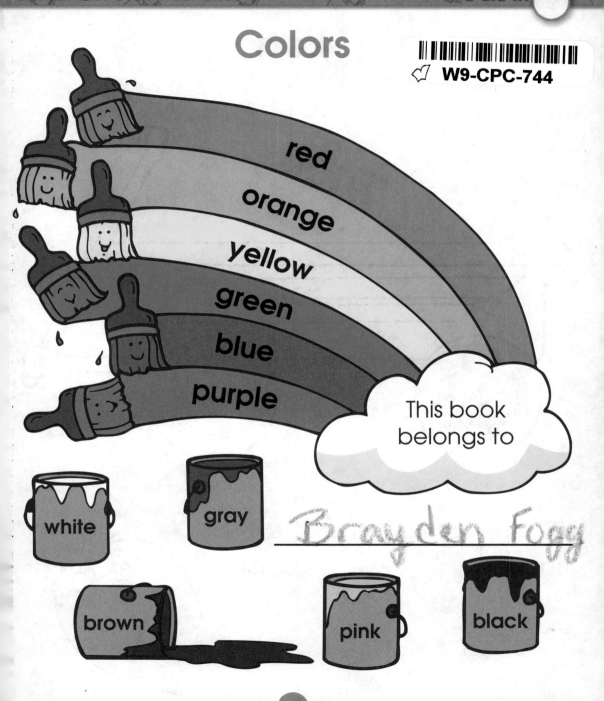

red

orange

yellow

green

blue

purple

This book belongs to

white

gray

brown

pink

black

Brayden Fogg

Red

Color the wagon **red**.

Trace.

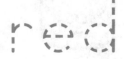

Color.

FS109010 • Colors

Red Things

Color the pictures **red**.

apple

stop sign

tomato

fire engine

3

You Choose

Color only the things that are **red**.

heart

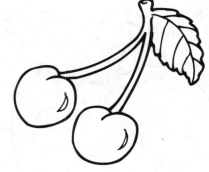

cherries

tiger

wagon

apple

house

FS109010 • Colors

Find Red Things

Color the **red** things **red**.

There are _____ **red** things.

5

FS109010 • Colors

Where Are the Apples?

Color all of the apples you can find **red**.

How many apples did you color? _____

FS109010 • Colors

Blue

Color the water **blue**.

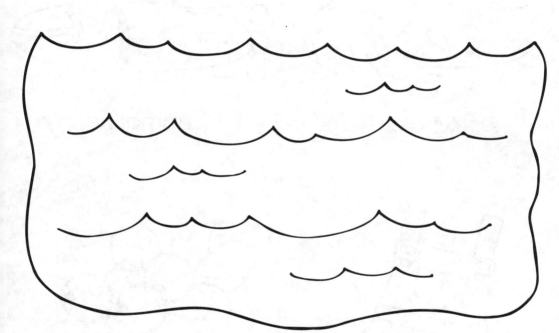

Trace.   Color.

FS109010 • Colors

Blue Things

Color the pictures **blue**.

whale

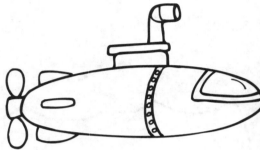

submarine

overalls

blueberries

FS109010 • Colors

What Is Blue?

Color only the things that are **blue**.

FS109010 • Colors

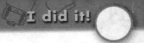

High in the Sky

Use the code to color the picture.

● = **blue**   ▲ = **red**

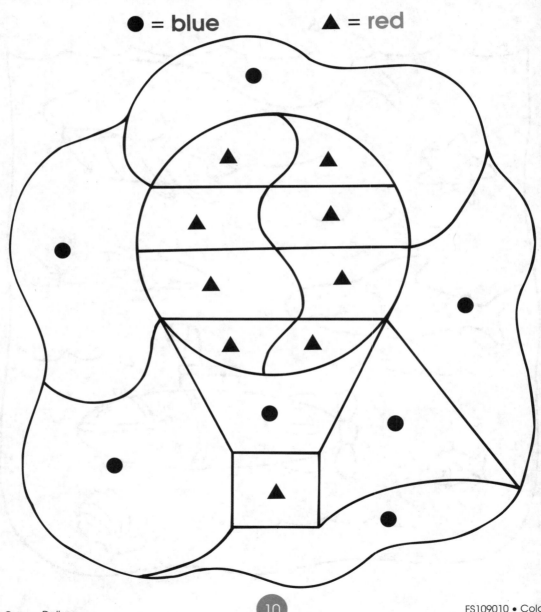

FS109010 • Colors

Hidden Blueberries

Find **6** blueberries ● hidden in the picture. Color them **blue**. Color the rest of the picture.

FS109010 • Colors

Yellow

Color the sun yellow.

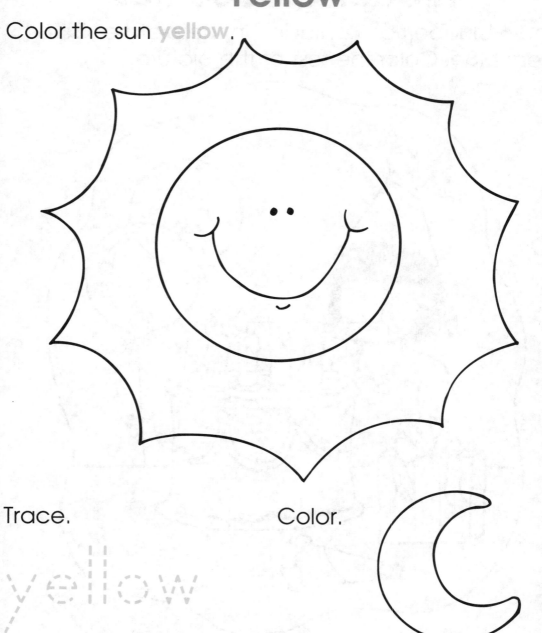

Trace.

yellow

Color.

Yellow Things

Color the pictures yellow.

lemon

star

bananas

duckling

13

You Decide

Color only the things that are yellow.

chick

rooster

bee

starfish

sun

dolphin

FS109010 • Colors

Yellow Fun

Color only the things that are yellow.

15

FS109010 • Colors

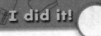

Crazy Maze

Color the yellow things to help Bailey find her crayons.

FS109010 • Colors

A Three-Color Creation

Use the code to color the picture.

▲ = red   ■ = yellow   ● = blue

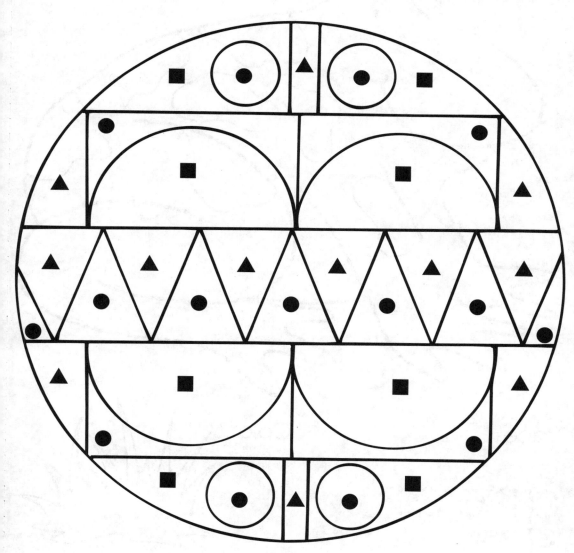

Green

Color the frog **green**.

Trace.

Color.

green

Green Things

Color the pictures **green**.

leaves

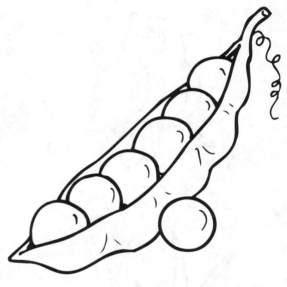

peas

broccoli

turtle

FS109010 • Colors

What Is Green?

Color only the things that are **green**.

owl

pickle

grass

leaf

bear

pig

FS109010 • Colors

Funny Frogs

Color all of the frogs green.

How many frogs did you color? _____

FS109010 • Colors

A Green Matchup

Draw **green** lines from the word **green** to the things that are **green**. Color the pictures.

Orange

Color the pumpkin orange.

Trace.

orange

Color.

FS109010 • Colors

Orange Things

Color the pictures orange.

fire

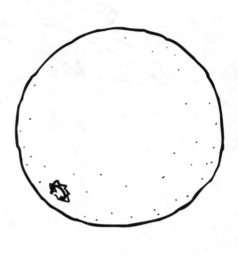

orange

pumpkin

carrot

Look for Orange Objects

Color all of the things that are orange.

FS109010 • Colors

Lucky Lindsay

Help Lindsay find the pumpkin patch. Color the pumpkins orange.

FS109010 • Colors

Crayons to Color

Read the words. Color the crayons.

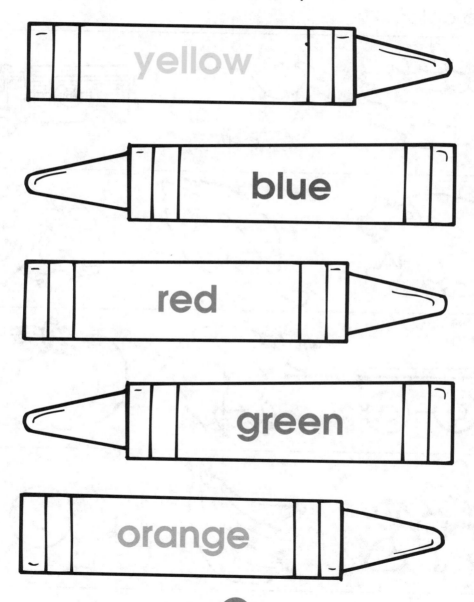

FS109010 • Colors

A Colorful Picture

In each row, color the two things that are the same color.

FS109010 • Colors

Purple

Color the grapes **purple**.

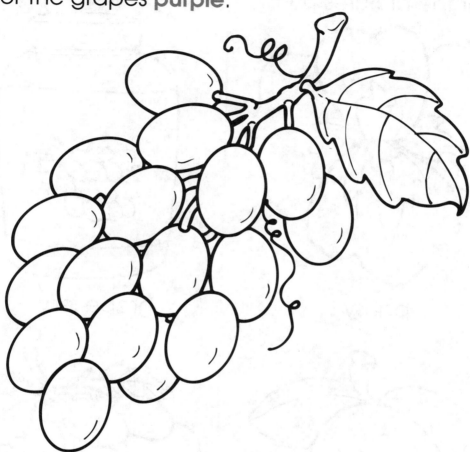

Trace.   Color.

purple

29   FS109010 • Colors

Purple Things

Color the pictures **purple**.

pansy

grape jelly

plum

grapes

Lunchtime

Color only the things that are **purple**.

FS109010 • Colors

Great Grapes

Joey wants grapes with his lunch. Help him find them. Color them **purple**.

Fly So High!

Use the code to color the picture.

▲ = **purple**   ● = yellow   ■ = **green**

FS109010 • Colors

Brown

Color the gorilla **brown**.

Trace.

b r o w n

Color.

FS109010 • Colors

Brown Things

Color the pictures **brown**.

trunk

owl

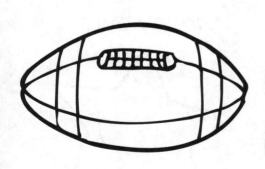

football

beaver

FS109010 • Colors

What Is Brown?

Color only the things that are **brown**.

gorilla

bananas

flower

teddy bear

gingerbread man

star

FS109010 • Colors

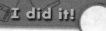

Look for Brown Things

Color only the things that are **brown**.

FS109010 • Colors

Brown and Yummy!

Use the code. Color the picture.

r = **red**

o = orange

b = **brown**

g = **green**

y = yellow

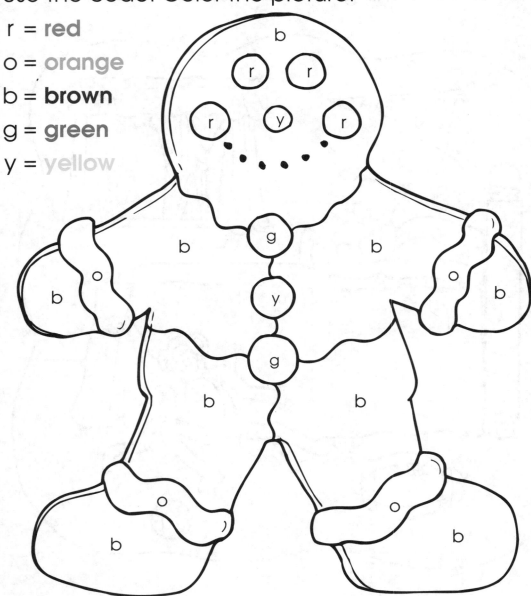

Black

Color the bat **black**.

Trace.

black

Color.

Black Things

Color the pictures **black**.

top hat

sea lion

ant

blackbird

Is Everything Black?

Color only the things that are **black**.

whale

tire

bat

wagon

frog

ant

What Is Black?

Color the black things **black**.

FS109010 • Colors

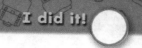

A Lost Wheel

Jason lost a wheel to his wagon. Color the objects that should be **black** to help him find it.

FS109010 • Colors

White

Color the snowman white.

Trace.

Color.

What's White?

Color only the things that are white.

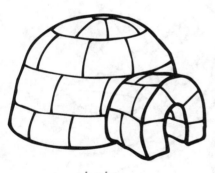

snowflake

apple

igloo

flower

dog

cloud

Pink

Color the rose pink.

Trace.

pink

Color.

Pink Things

Color the pictures pink.

flamingo

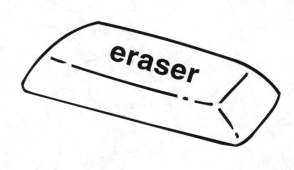

eraser

eraser

pig

rose

FS109010 • Colors

Perfectly Pink

Color the pink things pink.

FS109010 • Colors

Bright Balloons

Read the words. Color the picture.

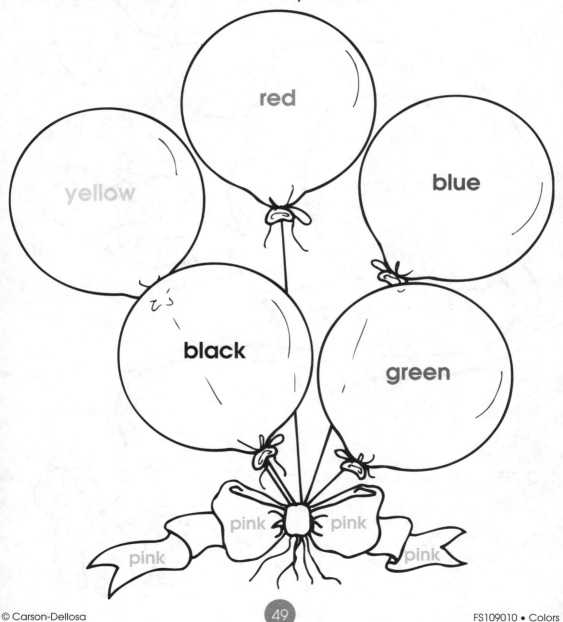

49

Gray

Color the mouse **gray**.

Trace.   Color.

© Carson-Dellosa   50   FS109010 • Colors

Gray Things

Color the pictures **gray**.

elephant

donkey

squirrel

mouse

Farmer Fred

Farmer Fred wants to catch the mice that are eating his grain. Find 5 mice hiding in the picture. Color them **gray**.

     FS109010 • Colors

Scared Ellie

Some people think that elephants are scared of mice! Help Ellie the elephant get away from the mouse and find her friends. Color the animals **gray**.

Color Fun

Match each picture to its crayon color. Color the pictures and the crayons.

red

blue

yellow

green

orange

More Color Fun

Match each picture to its crayon color. Color the pictures and the crayons.

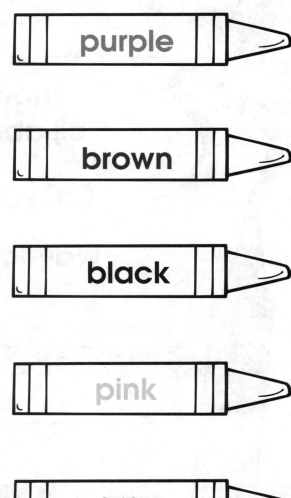

purple

brown

black

pink

gray

FS109010 • Colors

knows
all about

colors!

Way to go!

_____
signature

_____
date